ENDLESS THREATS

ENDLESS THREATS
POEMS

HANFORD YANG

PORTLAND • OREGON
INKWATERPRESS.COM

www.inkwaterpress.com

Paperback
ISBN-13 978-1-59299-391-8
ISBN-10 1-59299-391-5

Hardback
ISBN-13 978-1-59299-392-5
ISBN-10 1-59299-392-3

Publisher: Inkwater Press

Printed in the U.S.A.
All paper is acid free and meets all ANSI standards for archival quality paper.

1

To my mother
who nourished me with love.

To my governess, Ms. Lee
who protected me with wizardry.

Contents

Acknowledgment

With my younger brother Haner's trust and patience to assist me, these poems eventually were organized in an acceptable shape. The love and mutual respect are understood between us but rarely spoken. Thank you, Haner.

Other constructive advice and encouraging words are from: Karen Gunderson, Julian Weissman, Martha and Gamal El-Zoghby, Michael Price, Stephen Sanders, Yvonne C. Yang, Ginger Kwong, Amiel Vassilovski, C.H. Chung, S.Y. Chen, Michael Opest, Albert Wu, Michael Cary, Tony Marchese, Betty Y. Liu, Billy Jay Hoffman, my gratitude to all.

Introduction

In this, the first collection of poems to be published by Hanford Yang, we see an emerging synthesis of a poet's life in a society that has increasingly refused to lend itself to unifying theories or traditional artistic representation. Trained first in music and then in architecture, Mr. Yang's fields permeate his work. His observations are those of one who has spent a lifetime inspecting and listening, building and creating in the world around him. Here we find constant reference to a small litany of themes: the ever-cyclic habits of the natural world, distrust of artificial systems of knowledge, the forming and transforming powers of art, the vagaries of love, sexuality, and personal loss; and throughout, an acute sense of the ironies that pervade the everyday.

We see the first of these motifs in "Endless Threats" and "Beginning and End," where natural cycles are the only sureties available to us. "Prophecy, not logic, embraces fear, / Suffering, glory and financial gain," Yang writes in "Nature's Law." The comforts promised by religious metaphors cannot ultimately stand against natural forces. Despite the seeming coldness set up by his lack of faith, the world outside of our institutions can still be an anchor, a comfort even, as in "Change," where the narrator looks nightly to the shifting moon to balance his own self-doubts against his past and expectations. As in "Serenity," even peace can be found without the blind reference of belief.

"The exquisite serenity exists not in a / Society that obsesses with apocalypse."

Many of the pieces herein contain the expected experimentation with poetic form. A sonnet appears as the close of the four-part "Ode to Art," where the two equal stanzas work in the larger poem with the same function as the last two lines of a traditional Shakespearean sonnet. "A Day in SoHo" sees the distinct images of single haiku begin to build upon each other as the poem becomes a rather more extraordinary edifice, a self-contained haiku cycle. As Yang presents the banalities of daily life, their collective effect moves ironically toward a creeping, sinister commercialism, which, like shadows under skyscrapers, was always hiding behind benign images. That commercialism crops up again as the "indoctrinated ambitions," the workaday world of "Epigram in Five Parts," analogous to yet another false religion.

Beyond the pieces that work within those boundaries usually housed on the shelves of the Poetry section, many of Yang's poems echo and quote musical forms. In "My Happiness, My Pride," the author explicitly suggests reading with appropriate tempo, with an "Andante" like a stroll through the MoMA and a "Scherzo" that's as light as the sun reflected in a stream. "Four on Fog" presents impromptus that seem as improvised as anything one might add into a Chopin Fantasia, yet which are so crafted as to read like the seasons. Other poems beg to be read with the tripartite balance of a sonata, with variations in volume and pitch, or with an etude playing in the background.

These musical forms blend with similar quotations of architecture. Yang's formal studies with both Louis Kahn and Paul Rudolph respectively engendered keen senses of order and reason, lyricism and passion. "Four on Fog" flaunts its lyrical language just as its four parts might be analogous to columns supporting a portico. "Night Rain" offers further architectural lessons:

The rain dances on the car roof.
On the roof of the building, on my head.
Under the street lamp

Heavy drops burst into gold dust.
In the blackness
Everything glitters on the wet glass.

The sound of rain is love.
When all the lights are out,
Through the dark window panes
I see my eyes dancing
With wild markings on my face
By the constant rain.

The car, the building, the halo of the lamp all suggest the layers hiding behind a SoHo warehouse, from the hundred-year-old brick façade down to the brand new walls of a boutique's fitting room. Throughout the book we find reference to the interplay between large, open spaces and the personalized interior world. Indeed, the impetus for many poems lies in the reflection upon dichotomies of scale. So often, as again, in "Ode to Art," the largest of structures—the collective knowledge of art and its production—must rely on "private and furtive references."

Yang's work as an architect serves to frame the ideas at hand. One aspect of art braces another. With the mediating guide of the mind, art's power transforms the world: "From the humblest ingredients / Arts beg the hand of knowledge." Thus, in "A Night at Lincoln Center," the careful design of an atmosphere, coupled with the successes of artistic labor, serves to alter our human perception and understanding in a manner that vain religion never will.

Throughout the varied emphases on form, one notices the narratives never suffer. Nowhere is this more apparent than in the wistful poems that revolve around Yang's family. The only comfort of "Red Sweater," "Same Night," the close of "Epigram," and others is in the resolve to carry forward with life in spite of irrevocable loss, catastrophe, and squandered potential.

A pointed irony infuses his most personal works just as much as the more philosophical meditations. Quite often, the ironic urbanity in these poems provides the reader with a slight smile, as in the subject of "Civility," who, in an incautious insult, likens herself to a fly following shit. We also catch the spirit of such irony in his working method: "To design a house / I dream of castles in Spain / and what not to do." Perhaps, then, in turning the pages of this new collection, we might similarly put our minds elsewhere, and let the poems begin their true work from there.

– Michael Opest

Ode to Art

I. Inconceivable

By nature, art remains fast in an
Altruistic and extroverted result

By choice, art ideas oscillate with
Elusive, private and furtive references

By predilection, artists who select,
Indulge and personalize their convictions

Thus, essence of the artistic derives:
From the common—the uncommon.

Out of the conceivable—the
Most inconceivable.

II. Experiment

To view art—The prerequisites
Rest upon the participant's
Willing ear and receptive eye.

To know art—An extended heart and a
Reluctant tongue would accelerate the
Process of pleasure to differentiate.

To love art—The pledged affection
Propels a lifelong labor in which
To engage and to experiment.

The level of appreciation in art
Can't be measured by one's exclusion
From unschooled "likes and dislikes."

By discretionary inclusion of
All aspects of art, foster dedication,
Cultivation, experience, the eye matures.

Time, humility, generosity, perceptiveness,
Persistence, passion……may all bear
Seeds to view, to know and to love art.

III. Original
(To Yayoi Kusama)

Road to recognition has paved tribulation.
Confronting art, two extra hurdles yet to cross:
To unchain from endemic and academic boundary
To survive time's appraisal and selections.

What is good art? What is not?
Sovereign knowledge clears not the equivocality.
Tide bends the yardstick to measure. But in a
Ceaseless toil of making, good art is near.

Ability to judge arrives late.
Long after you've buried all the
Textbooks and your words are
Free from ostentation, yet original.

IV. A Sonnet
(In memory of Dick Bellamy)

Art lights the impossible
Art expresses the undeniable
Art exists in war and peace, in good and evil,
Dwelling on concept and in details.
Art sings to sunrise, sunset,
Thunder, flower, tiger, spider
And the birth and the death.

Art welcomes and unfolds to change
But refuses to be fashionable.
Art is a judge seeking the truth. The
Excellence of the old and new may never perish.
Art is art is art is art.
Without art, man is incomplete
And the universe is less poetic.

A Day in SoHo

SoHo never sleeps
When the drunks go home at dawn
The garbage truck cometh.

Funny morning birds
All rush here to decode last
Night's untold secrets.

Lilac in a vase—
Greets me in my studio
With faith and good smell.

To design a house
I dream of castles in Spain
And what not to do

First rain in two weeks
Plants laughing as they sip
The afternoon "Tea."

My sister phones
Same topic with another view
Old age, nothing new.

A noisy sunset.
A musical potpourri
Of cars, dogs, birds, wind......

After a quick bite,
It's my evening with Bach and
Bach and Bach and Bach......

In paint-splattered jeans
Euro jocks postulate
SoHo arty scene.

Drink from plastic cup
Crowds jostle for attention
At art openings.

Approaching midnight
Coy, circumspecting sleep
Guards my pillows.

Nightmares don't scare me.
Dream riding on old deeds—
Be wrong but not evil.

SoHo changes its tune
When boutiques crash the street
Art withdraws its voice.

(After Haiku)

Endless Threats
(for Paula Cooper)

The sky stays navy blue,
In dusty yellow, the crescent moon engages
A tug of war over the night's on-time departure,
Knowing the coming of day ends her allotted liberty.

One by one, the obedient stars abscond.
A sudden wind breaks the silence from
Drowsy colors among the summer trees.
In the violet dew struggles a new dawn.

The morning steps out fresh 'n breezy,
A tug of war over the low land fog
Has declared victorious. Now,
The sky stays fire engine red.

The narcissistic sun rises slow 'n in luxury.
Shrouded by a lofty trail of diamond 'n ruby...
Its blinding rays cast long shadows over the
Fertile landscape which refuses to be regimented.

By 'n by, time negotiates a peaceful passage,
The birds 'n bees bicker over their daily chores.
Perceptibly, the heated sky swirls to a maniacal threat.
The frightened sun tugs with angry clouds in vain.

Then,
A storm.
Then,
A young twilight oscillates.

New York

Times Square at night
Blossoms with life and colors
An urban spring.

A poetic morning
Empty beach in summer rain. Crowds
Come when it's perfect.

Shades of autumn
Reprise on the tree, wind, rain,
Between my eyebrows.

City's first snowstorm
Smoothed sidewalk's crack, but
None on wall's graffiti.

(After Scriabin Etude, B minor, op. 8, no. 11)

Change

Looking into the night sky,
I find the moon missing.
A few stars blinking through
the black void strive to refine
the outline of scattered clouds.

Without moon as a reference, my pride to identify
objects in the sky turns discombobulated.

The moonless night conjures up the
devilish scares of a Hollywood
B movie. But, under the quiet moon,
it inspires me to ask myself:
"Did you forgive you?"

As sure as my best friend,
the shape may alter, the moon'll return,
if not by tomorrow night, the night after.

But, it'll occupy another time, another space.

Time or space proceeds without instinct, unaware that—
my anguish won't be the same,
my feeling on "the night after" may change.

Four on Fog
(4 Impromptus)

I. Entrance

The dense fog
Of N.Y.C. in January
Shrouds
The ostentatious skyscrapers
In this morning to an
Indefinable silhouette of grey.
The yellow cab's
Blurring headlights
Prompt
My entrance alone to face
The scenery-altered city.
Like in a monochromatic art movie
With countless murky images
Race
By me, featuring the
Fog's irascible metamorphosis.

II. Choppy Waters

The bewitching fog
Of San Francisco in May
Boasts
Nature's artistic indulgence
The romantic spell casts
A sensuous net by the bay.
We meet while catching
The ferry to visit Alcatraz. We
Touch, kiss
Oblivious to the choppy waters.
Never again to meet,
Time has grayed my hair.
Her warm lips quietly
Return
To mine, whenever the
Chilly fog advances.

III. Crackling

The persistent fog
Of Chungking in October
Ascends
From the meeting of its two rivers
An ennui, but town folks accept it
As an unavoidable friend,
At dawn, in the school yard,
Standing with precision, we
Stretch, squat
In boy scout's uniform following
The recorded instruction from
A crackling loudspeaker.
With great verve and gusto, we
Respond
In patriotic 1234, 1234
In the innocent, frosty fog.

IV. Curtain

Respighi's musical fog
Binds pines and Rome.
Pollock's volatile fog
Suggests a tint of lavender.
T.S. Eliot's sly fog
Withholds intrigues more than Sandburg's.
Fog's appearance accentuates
The beauty 'n danger.
Fog's temperament accentuates
The constant 'n ephemeral.
Fog's destiny accentuates
The predictability 'n mystique.
Like a shower curtain
Fog shields me with privacy.
I nudge myself to laugh
At yesterday's despair.

Night Rain

The rain dances on the car roof,
On the roof of the building, on my head.
Under the street lamp
Heavy drops burst into gold dust.
In the blackness
Everything glitters on the wet glass.

The sound of rain is love.
When all the lights are out,
Through the dark window panes
I see my eyes dancing
With wild markings on my face
By the constant rain.

Night Rain (2)

That persistent even tune is
Not a Chopin nocturne
Played by candlelight,
But the hoofing sound of a tired horse
Seeking company in a dark field.
Night rain, melancholy and wretched is
Intentionally wrestled away
From my dream.

Raised among comforts
Early I chased my American Dream.
Ready, like a pumped-up soldier
On the charge.

Mother was quiet when it was time
She knew my travels would be long
The parting was final.

Touching her hands, I saw
Her face trembled with
Unwitting wetness, a rain
Brushing flower petals.

My Happiness, My Pride
(Three Lyric Pieces)

1. Allegro—Eyes

If your
Winning expectation
Overshadows my
Remnant pride
Consider the
Happiness from
Your assiduous eyes
Unctuous.

Thus, my
Agony from
Our winless happiness
Has cued
Me to
Spring up
With pride and
Metastasize.

II. Andante—Irrefutable

My happiness resides in the museum
A conversation there with my intimates
Brings the inquisitive, languid ritual.
Their sorrow 'n happiness
Prescribed aloud in public.
Their sorrow 'n happiness
Inscribe on me without embellishment.
Their worldwide recognitions incite
The refutable critic's concocted debate.
Their unfathomable images demand
The irrefutable honor in prints.
Raised above the floor like wall fixtures.
Self-conscious, immobile, silent,
They submit to the unavoidable glare,
The enmity of jeer and envy.
But, my love 'n fidelity have been adopted by them
So irrevocably that our acknowledgment needs
But a surreptitious nod.

III. Scherzo—Synchronization

My pride holds but few obsessions. Not from
Wall Street, nor my old published works, the
Winding stream near my house counts as one---a
Walk to meditate, a spot to observe fish. If luck
Strikes, the leader might raise her golden head.
"Thanks for the lunch. We can't sing your favorite
Art songs by Tosti, Sir." She says: "Came from
Upstate, we'll perform our native dance."

1. Flip 'n a twist.
2. Flip 'n a twist.
3. Flip 'n a twist.

"An athletic tail helps. The trick lies in the
Synchronization between flips and the gurgles in
A stream," she says. My pride takes over. "I'm no
Gigli, nor Domingo, Madame." I say: "Came from
The other side of the globe, let me
Rehearse a bit. Tomorrow, I'll bring my
Er-Hu to entertain you in Chinese tune."

Seattle

Seattle stands in September's rain
Glass towers dwarf the old brick town
In a predawn windy sky
Olympic Mountains gently sway.

Over green hills, reddened apples
Hang with spotted mud.
Surf in blue mist, fishing boats'
Mournful whistles greet the sleepy shore.

We say good-bye with quiet words.
My visit, regrettably, is forty years late.
Joyful college memories sting our faces
Unaware, frost has coated the near rose.

Time won't listen to unfulfilled dreams,
Against all the tempestuous struggles, the sun rises.
Traffic speeds along a tangled highway
Like soldiers' precision drills on parade—

Quick slow, slow quick......
My eyes trail the calls of the migratory bird
Afar, in its full splendor
The silvery airport flashes welcoming beams.

Nature's Law

Consider not it a cultural resentment
Nor an uncouth mental blind over
Matters so clear but unreasonable.

I'm not offended by nature's arrogance.
To decode its unknown, compounded fables
Clarify less its magnificence.

Things strategically revealed, reveal in percentage.
The choice between belief or disbelief
Plays a mind game in chronology.

I'm not tempted to outwit nature's way.
Prophecy, not logic, embraces fear,
Suffering, glory and financial gain.

Like a summer romance, or a snowstorm or
A long lost visit to my hometown, the finality of
One life brings back another bittersweet cycle.

Yes, I'm bewildered by nature's ambiguity.
The sky shuts down—expands.
Water produces—yet kills.

Traveling with a sealed agenda,
Rich or poor, big and small, everybody, everything
Is listed "on time," according to nature's law.

A Success

Memory is a private matter
that contains secrets, which are
good but bitter, sweet maybe evil.

No rules or regulations are applied.
Memory is mostly exaggerated or
tailored or fabricated like a fairy tale.

To lie is a moral issue.
To offend is a legal issue.
The difference between a biography 'n
an autobiography is that in the latter,
the truths and lies are narrated
directly from the horse's mouth.

Memory is a selective confession which
discards the unfavorable in the process.
A murder attracts more than death by
old age. Who blindfolded the ethical code?
Who wants to hear a bore rehash his
dull memory?

The writers are encouraged—
to garnish the fact,
to omit the guilt,
to be a hero,
to be a jerk.
Be belligerent.
Be generous.
Be colorful and cool.
Be lustful and cruel.

And—
That is rated as a commercial success.

Farm for Sale

Halfway up the hill
The farmhouse is surrounded by
A barn, a stable and a storage bin
With a corrugated tin roof.
The late autumn sun bathes the house
On its 20 acres of rugged land.

The landlord is a rugged man
With sharp green eyes set
Deep in his bald head.
An ex–Wall Street stockbroker
With his quick wits and dare
He made big killings on the market
Retired from the wheeling and dealing at 38
To a world of nature, beauty and solitude.
Now, after 5 years,
The farm is for sale
Seeing that the developments are encroaching.

We sip mixed drinks on the veranda
The hills cast long shadows to each other.
A red hawk glides along the willowy stream.
A family of deer rustle among
The knee-high yellow straws.
The stars begin to glow in the purple sky.
Silence has descended on everything
Except the softness of Mozart's piano music
Coming through the unlit living room.

Lost

Lost in the blur of air
The autumn sun
Shook brilliant colors
As the leaves
Flipped and twisted.

A surreal calm sustains the city.
The buildings stand with
Unabashed dignity and perverse pride.
Beneath a blackness of rain
Flowers quiver on the wet ground.

Studio spotlight accents my inner chagrin.
I design, teach, work
With joyless contentment.
Oh, do not look into my eyes.
All the love letters in
My head are paling to illegibility.

Ramification

From the good
genius of Shakespeare
and Verdi
who intensified love's
promise and deceit
of Otello

into a lesson
from which we
can examine
our own love's
twisted entitlement
and its ramification.

A Red Sweater

A proclaimed pragmatist
My sister Betty rarely shed tears on
Matters she considered trivialities.
But, when Puccini's *La Bohème*
Engulfed her, she cried unabashedly
Not for Mimi's love's lost but her
Fatal falling into love.

I am an obstinate romanticist
Acquired taste in melodrama, moonlight stroll,
Wild leopards and Schubert's Impromptus......
A love story like *La Bohème* is common
But I admired Colline's cavalier in vain gesture
In parting his great coat to save Mimi.

One day, with an expression like a flower
Willing to be entrapped by love
Betty cried unabashedly
Meeting an adventurer from Australia
During a Moonlight stroll in Hong Kong,
She forsook her career, her friends
And family to be the best slave of love
And followed him "down under"
To have babies.

One Christmas, a red sweater
Knitted by Betty arrived
Along with news of two sons
Her husband had settled down
Both of them gained weight.

The days go by
The red sweater is now out of shape,
Fifteen years old, the faded wool is wearing thin.
Due to her failing eyesight
Betty has stopped sewing and knitting.
In a disturbance of cool days
Among all other fine wools I possess,
Her gift still gives me
The most comfort.

Fortunately, I have no opportunity
To test the cavalier gesture
In *La Bohème.*

A Letter

Dear father,
What a strange feeling of loneliness
Possessed me in this grey morning
And I consider again writing to you.
Writing means trust
To be totally free and honest.
Then, perhaps you may finally understand
My view of life, my melancholy,
My devotion to nature's beauty
To live free from ostentation.
I am an idealist, as you said,
Chasing goals not given to me.

Different as it is, I could never share your
Pride in brute force.
Each of your sons and daughters has his own being.
But, honesty or friendly discussion always
Turned our peaceful existence to rage.

Followed by guilt, regrets, humiliation......
So, we lived in pretense
Exchanged eternal platitudes.
Now, it's too late, a big void without you.
To be honest with you, father,
I have never been honest with you
And that might be the most sensible
Of all approaches.

To Iris

In the grey ridges of Central Park
Swallows ride the soft air
With a bewitching color
A conceptual art.

Fifth Avenue crowds surge
To see to be seen, eager primped maiden
Splash an artificial scent
Decoration of flower of silk, scentless.

Warm wind brings out
Cheering signals of April
Presumptuous flowers are everywhere;
Countless variations of shape, color and smell.

And, there is Iris, that noble color
Of the brightest purple
Blanketing my family garden
Come Spring.

Near the Woods

"In Viet-Nam, I learned the soldier's way.
Upon my return, I longed to live
Near the woods with birds and streams.
First, I had to slave for years
To find this place."

"And at last you've found your dream!"

"Well, not quite, when I first moved in.
There was this damn woodpecker
Making a tick, tick, tick noise
On that metal roof of the silo and
Woke me up every morning at six.
After a week,
I took out my .45
And blasted that poor thing to bits."

Christmas Light

St. Patrick's bells are ringing.
The blue sky shines from
Your eyes to my eyes.
Beginnings are always worrisome.

My father died a lady's man at 96.
He taught me about power and position
But nothing about love.
I seek shelter when passion knocks,
Fear the repeats of hurt
That my Mother endured......
This time it feels right.

In an Italian restaurant
We touch hands
At a subway entrance
Our lips meet.
You rush to the train,
Home by plane to Phoenix.
I watch the colored Christmas lights dim
One by one, on your snow-like hair.

My Sister

After the children are fed,
Bathed, tucked in bed,
Dishes washed, floor swept,
Toys gathered in closet;

After her husband yawned,
Folded newspaper,
Scratched himself,
Closed bedroom door;

My sister turns to me
And shuts her eyes,
"Well, this is the general measure of
How a day in my life is spent."

Quickly she gets up
Checking if the doors are locked,
Oven switched off,
Laundry out of the dryer,
Dog and cat are in,
Then turns off the light.

A Form

A form, which is complex yet clear.
A mountain cave,
A bird's nest,
Space within space
Walls breathing air.

A color, which is bright and pure,
An autumn leaf,
An opal ring,
Mutable as blue sky's fluffy clouds
Altering white to pink and gold
When sun slips below.

A sound, which is soft but original.
A Bach fugue
A Schubert song,
Spring wind, water running
In a rocky stream.
Melodious and reticent,
Resonates my mother's discretional words.

What secret lies in my heart?
What echoes in my dream?
Hope, strife, fly,
Move on within this form,
Bathing by this color and sound.

A Mission

All flowers are beautiful.
Each flower has a mission.
Each particular scent or color or
shape is a weapon, no ...a seducer.

Those who are rewarded with food have
agreed to be flower's messenger of love.

The mountain snow offers nutrient in the
clear stream where wild daisies 'n lilies drink.
By the rocky cliff, blue forget-me-nots wait
twice daily for the sea's gratuitous visits.

Some flowers are medicine.
Some flowers provide love potions.
Some manufacture colors to inspire artist,
cosmetologist, couturier, even fireworks.
Some become needed shelters for tiny friends.

We buy cut flowers to alleviate our dreariness,
or to wrap them in plastic,
as gift to express love or pretext, or as
a sycophantic investment of chance.

In a quiet moment, from a vase,
I hear the flowers sobbing:
"Our mission unfulfilled. Now,
we die twice to give pleasure
to so few, so quickly."

Spring

Two hawks hurry in breaking snow
Overwhelmed by witnessed miracle—
Their two nestling mute eggs break into
Four close eyed, hungry, noisy brood.

Punctual as spring flowers, diligent as a brook,
Beak to beak, they tend the young fastidious morsels.
Tip to tip, they stretch the feathery arms to
Form the eyes for things perceived and unperceived

Care dwells in heart's deepest chamber
Carrying love, blind and binding.
Anguish dreams, simple and singular,
Encompass the progeny's swift shadows skyward

Summer

Dawn interrupts sun's ritual bath
In the placid purple sea.
Reddened with displeasure, sun billows
His golden torso in thunderous roars.

Obsequious waves flaunting their loyalty
Smash relentless fists against a blameless shore
Shake minute creatures in foamy sand,
Armored neighbors all bolted tight.

Shore birds' songs soften the jittery mood,
Hesitant sky gazes mist away,
Gusty wind scoops sand to waltz,
Prompting dune grasses to whistle.

Behind a shadowy ravine forensic evidence
Suggests, in chaotic footprints a struggle.
Loose feathers on stained ground
An ambush before dawn.

Autumn

Too late for daffodils
Too early for the snow
Chill winds shorten orioles' visit. Impetuous
Color betrays the generous maple tree.

As if an ominous curse has
Been dispelled from the north
Tension displays a strangle-hold
From dew to the tremulous stream.

From brown lips of grass
Discontentment is heard that
The wild rain of withered leaves obstinately
Blots out the already dimmed sun.

Under the stupendous and reproachful sky
Butterfly, spider, bees, ants all hurry home.
Save the diligent squirrel gathering
Treasures just to bury them.

Autumn quivers through pensive clouds to
Warn my winding path ahead be precarious
Therefore, I be gathering as a squirrel.
Therefore, I be giving as the maple.

December

Fickle are the last days of December

As if designated by the calendar
Civility extends a helping hand
To open the umbrella of decency
Love is read in a hundred ways.

Thousands of bells are ringing
Millions of colored lights are blinking
With infinite care, the city's seasonal
Metamorphosis is lavishly complete—

Striking as a majorette with a brand new beat (to)
Snap, sing, swing in vintage tunes
Insist on shops to reveal their irretrievable romances
Crowds surge and gawk like migratory seals.

'Tis the season the faithful pray for paradise
'Tis the hour the merry makers drink to the new
Nothing changes, when clock strikes at twelve
But the trampled confetti tottering into silent night.

Unforgiving are the last days of December

All things created—grow old.
Older still the day after
Science gears up to master immortality—
"Fountain of Youth" is a fleeting dare.

Mayflies live but a day. The sun
Too will close its cosmic door.
Incomprehensible is time's roster. Trust,
He be the fairest judge.

"Oh, your honor," I said.
"Hear me. I'm down.
"The long journey has been tumultuous.
"Please ignore my being tardy and grey,

"I just begin to search and
"I just begin to like me.
"I just begin to
"Like me."

Love

Love stirs up a storm and
Drenches every minute part of
My body with hope

Hope swells me with the confidence of desire,
Like a lightning stroke, its tongue aims
At your heart with salacious fire.

Fire monopolizes, or else,
The flame incinerates all
That's been proclaimed.

Yet——

Proclaimed "Ashes of passion" from
Old flames give nourishments
To deflated hope

Hope, in time,
Locates the key
To new love.

New love stimulates with new games—
Quick smile, small talks, long kisses. The
Coded action falls back to the path of old love.

Yet——

Old love, new love, love is all, is love all?
Be there always storm and lightning.
Be there no fire, if gone, desire.

Sunflowers
(To van Gogh)

The sunflowers in the field
Innumerable and riotous, on them,
Rain and rainbow accentuate a golden shine.

Their corn-colored hair is dressed as bonnets
Their black eyes recognize the proud telling sound—
Prelude to a bountiful summer.

Eager morning raised the curtain of vermillion haze,
Purplish green stretches across the hills and
Unrolls the French village like a Japanese print.

Powdery blossoms in tender pink and yellow
Vie for reclaiming the fruit orchards. An icy winter
Has debilitated the rain-drenched plateau.

An old river supplies the draw-bridge with daily exaltation,
A flock of rambling birds chant in confidence—
When sunflowers turn toward the sun, food is everywhere.

Again, nature presents us a state of restitution and wonder.
Can we cherish its consecrated beauty
Without routing it with our less sterling ambitions?

Seized by the sensuous color of yellow,
Van Gogh immortalizes the fragile, yet defiant
Portraits of the "flower of the sun"—

Like the ones of his full-throttled own.

Wind

By morning, the sun steps out in its full magnificence.

So sharp, I see
The snappy autumn wind
Chiseled the morning clouds
Into biomorphic creatures.
White costumed in blue air
Proceed to transfix and transmute
Divine as they desire to be—
A multitude of solid, porous,
Abstract, representational,
Peculiar, hilarious lot.
All jostle for recognition as dancers
To an endemic magic show.

So harsh, I hear
The horrid autumn wind
Growls at the decorous dancers
Misinterprets their graceful movements
As spiritless choreography.
Push and pull, recede and repose
He proceeds to sponsor
A new zany production.
Oh, poor timid dancers
Overstep in panic, trip, bump,
Collide in chaos
Suffer in disgust and tears!

So distressing, I fear
The deranged autumn wind
Unleashes his unfathomable rage,
Smashing with drum-like fists,
Slashing with blinding metallic whip,
Preoccupied with curse and vituperation.
Absent of logic or pride,
Demolishes all that he has fostered,
Slighting gentle sun's plea
To bring back harmony,
The wind's torrid screams and profanity
Won't subside when evening descends.

By night, neither moon, nor stars rush to shine.

(After Chopin Nocturne, C minor, op.48, no. 1)

Civility

She yells
Angrily
At him—

"Mediocre people
Prefer
Mediocre things

Like a
Fly
Follows shit."

Story of Waves

Bright and smooth as a ballroom floor
Colors rich as June's flower market.
With the least provocation, however; waves
Laugh cynically and churn the sea to a boil.

Each wave is new at sea.
Although endowed with similar traits
Waves upon waves
Each one's detail is unique.

Born in the water-world's pandemonium,
Like orphans who endure cruel indifference.
Waves learn to be waves
To be irascible, gentle, recalcitrant all at once.

Seeking guidance, perhaps usefulness
Embracing life's complexity and contradiction
To face a world of ingenuity and waste
Destiny leads waves escaping from the sea.

Alas! One by one, waves after waves,
Some beach like whales in silence!
Others end by smashing
Against the rocky cliff.

Interpretation of the Moon

J: "Oh, look at that moon, perfect and bright.
   It's a great night to try night-flying
   So free and cool, such a charge,
   Something adventurous."

F: "Look at our shadows reflected by
   The moonlight criss-crossed on the pond
   So mysteriously fragmented.
   Something magical."

J: "I enjoy looking up into the sky.
   The stars, the galaxy, expanding universe—
   So inspirational if comprehended. And that's
   My predilection."

F: "But-look close, from deep down and within.
   It might not alter history or climate, but
   So fulfilling, if the moon would incite the voice in
   My poetry."

Beautiful

They say to say a thing is beautiful is a cliché
That that word is overused
Too general, too simple, tacky!
Only bad writer repeats it.
Smart critics always condemn it
That saying a thing is beautiful
Is saying nothing. "Un-poetic."

Yet—

Yet every time I stand before Rothko's paintings
The word "Beautiful" floats around me.
I can hear this word reverberating
I can touch it in my brain,
Taste it without grandiloquence.
Because of his work hanging there,
I feel the room becomes beautiful

And my world seems more so,
After I learn and walk from it.

(After Chopin Etudes, A flat major, op.25, no. 1)

Reoccurring Dialogue
(Sonata in three movements)

Allegro...

"Yes, but it's—untrue." He says.
"No, but it's—true." She says.

"It's funny. I remember nothing."
"It's sad. Confusing insipience and innocence."

"Come on, let's forgive and forget."
"Go away, not to a repeated offender."

Andante...

"But I'm still in love with you."
"And I'm still psychosomatic to these words."

"You?"
"I!"

"Damn it all---"
"Damn you—Damn you."

Rondo..

"Well?—" He says.
"——" She says.

"Well? **Well?**" He says.
"___" She says.

"——" He says.
"**Well! Well! Well!**" She says.

Early Snow

So voracious is the storm, unexpected
For mid-November. An arctic
Maniacal fit un-negotiable alters my
Pastoral view through the living room.

30 hours long, 12" high
The unbounded snow
Blankets the parkland to
A pristine abandonment.

Silence, tension builds behind amity.
Time-thermodynamics-accord has passed its
Partisan rhetoric in dealing with
The nature's ephemeral new birth. Still,

The frozen air, obdurate and petulant,
Forbids the entry of any garden visitors
Whose wayward footprints
Would decidedly spoil the

White, soft, novel pavement.
By 4 p.m. low in the pink sky
The sun gives an abridged audience.
Paler, equivocally, apologetically

"His Majesty" endures the blame on this
Unseasoned re-scheduling—a contretemps
If not a near calamity?
If not a divine comedy?

A Guide and a Star

It enters your mouth with a touch of bitterness
Your nose discloses a lucid fragrance
The soft sweetness at once teases your tongue
Your body is comforted, your mind enters
Into a state of involuntary contentment.

Mr. Shu's "Flower Tea" reaches out—
Fame comes by word of mouth—like miracles.
Like snowflakes fluttering in a jade pond, the
Jasmine's white petals accentuate the pale green drink.
The flowers are hand picked, the tea holds secret to brew.

Coffee or tea? A debate no more, but a commitment.
I'm up with a cup of the "Flower Tea."
A cup before the work begins
A cup during lunch and
A cup during tea time at 4 p.m.

Another cup when I dine and another after......
Whiskey, vodka, beer or soda pop, none toasts me
Good wishes on health and happiness. Yet, when I dream,
Mr. Shu corresponds with my smile.
His tea is decidedly a guide and a star.

Fantasia Sketch
(To Vivaldi)

Spring exudes romance
He prefers Beethoven's passion
She craves Debussy's moonlight

Summer races by
In his lascivious kisses
She hears goodbyes

Autumn solicits resolve
She demands space
He declines time

Winter obscures objectives
She supports *A Doll's House*
He harbors *Carmen*

Ten Easy Pieces

I

The motivation of love
Expounds an unresolved impulse
Which shapes the unconsciousness—
A mandatory one,
Like living or dying.

II

Spring accumulates my desire
Summer spills my prospects
Autumn laden with our discontent
Winter's tale of our unreachable regret.

III

Kusama's art brings about
A stirring narrative of pain
An inflicted madness
A marginalization of art establishment
And it pricks.

IV

At dawn
I feel old age
Embracing me.

V

From the busy streets,
Alone, I found the root of all
Schubert's sorrows.

VI

Your unrelenting melancholy exposes
A biographical source of secrets,
A summoned indifference,
Or the silent defenders of love that
Resonate into unreasonable reasons.

VII

If I die,
Unloading all my loneliness to God
Am I still a good boy?

If I live
Gaining all my goodness from God
Can I still be my own man?

VIII

Poor architect!
Building others' dream houses
But not his own.

IX

First day of May
Tranquil spring and communists
Honor my birthday.

X

In my mother's world
My father ruled with tyranny
And scandals.

In my mother's eyes
I saw my father's
Fierce hand.

In my mother's heart
Father's constant absence
Dulled all her dreams.

In my mother's retreat
Roads planned in details to win
But, faithful heart won.

In my mother's release
Holding a broken heart
She beamed with relief

Against fateful ills
Rose above wrangles 'n betrayal
She sought but fairness

A wife's love inspires
A mother's love nurtures
Mother, all your love shines

Wink

The shape of a broken-heart
Displayed rarely in broken pieces.
Invisibly, the wound sinks in slow
To deplete the nucleus of your soul.

The cry from a surrendered mind
Often connotes with multi-colors.
Green for greed, red-lust, black-jealousy,
For truth, let transparency be?

Takes pride, a philosopher to infuse the
Words of solace in his abstruse metaphor.
In tedium, a psychiatrist's therapy hinges
On the "regression to your childhood."

No writer feels short to fabricate, nor a
Poet vacillates between indulging and ignoring.
Can a friendship rendered without trade or
A mother's love that deadens all pains?

Let the epoch spring to reclaim! With the
Replenished voice propels your cautionary eyes
Looking into an ampler mirror, pamper, flatter,
And reward yourself an all-knowing wink.

Same Night

The unrelenting heat closes the day
August wind incites the western sky ablaze.
Falling fast, the vanquished sun clinches on
Horizon's brim as the sea churns to a fury.

The evening chant breaks out in the sand dune. Tiny
Musical creatures tune in phraseless compositions—
Quiet as a meditation, loud as a riot, confidential
As sighs and shouts of struggle and despair.

All the sea birds've abandoned the panicked sky
Save a single gull to ride the darkened air,
Its moans lodge in my mind of bereavement
Its shadow burns my eyes with punishment.

Same night, twenty years ago, my mother was buried.
Bedridden from a stroke, she suffered for years
Of negligence and disdain from those she trusted,
While her children were across the ocean.

Mother's passing left me in insurmountable desolation.
I clinched, shouted, moaned in silent remembrance.
After the funeral, cutting into his hearty dinner,
My uncle turned to me:

"But your tears didn't flow like your sister's."

Dance

Miracle follows just a fraction of you.
Touching a decrepit plant, flowers bloom
Dancing with clouds, rainbow fills the lake full.

The song of night is clearly visible.
Firefly leads the path to where tiny singers
Profess of love in foreign rhythm and syllable.

Truth is an exploitation of fractured logic.
Let me mask over my implausible past and
The frenzied single-minded pursuit of possibilities.

No lugubrious words on my September trek.
In alliance with songs of foreignness, my secret
Awaits a fraction of miracle's touch and dance.

To Reiterate

To reiterate the riddle between love and passion
The eternal irony imperceptibly unfolds:

Love is now and forever.
Passion is now or maybe never.
Love renews through dedication.
Passion refreshes through multiplication.

To love is to give——a surrender of you
For passion it's to take—a conquest by you
For love——less is "more."
To passion—more is "more or less."

Supplied by a copious heart,
Love caresses with tender eyes.
Dominated by a lascivious mind,
Passion stalks with jealous hands.

Breathless,
Be as love-lorn as a Romeo,
Blindness,
Be as passion-crazed as an Othello

Oh! Constrains man,
What noble logic to die for love!
Uh! Betrays man,
What evil consult to kill for passion!

But——But——

Love with passion is a great love.
Love without passion is a bore.
Passion with love is a great steal.
Passion without love is a chore.

Love searches like a song's melody
Which carries words of longing and solace.
Passion struggles like the song's composer
Who reaches its goal in spite of the madness.

Love is a flower
Passion is its nectar
Love is the nectar's supplier
Passion is the flower's drunken bee.

L. says, "I love you."
P. says, "I want you."
L. says, "I want to love you."
P. says, " Let me facilitate your wanting to love."

But——But——

To reiterate the riddle between love and passion,
A ritualistic valor best be locked in its folds.

(After Chopin Etudes, E flat, op. 10, no. 11)

Serenity

The perceived serenity will never be attained,
If a lifestyle overtly exaggerates its direction.
Neither medical nor technological edge can help.
Enough said about conventional wisdom,
Regardless how scintillating with exultation.

This may sound like a kind of new theology.
We hear about love, but can't always see it.
The spiritual enlightenment is bestowed
Upon the analytical inquisitor who
Trusts rationality more than exotic myth.

The exquisite serenity exists not in a
Society that obsesses with apocalypse.
The truth is in the compiled telescopic data of
Our planetary system. With air, water, bees, flowers,
How comforting! Earth is indeed the heaven

The universe is still a work in progress.
Neither seer nor prayer, but the scientists who bear
The burden to prove the meticulosity of its creation.
With graceful energy, melancholy resilience,
Because the mighty sun is up there, we are here.

The ultimate serenity—A nature's grand gift
To those who embrace everything
Impose nothing.
Evoke everyone
Envy no one.

Street Philosophers

Times Square turns boisterous as
The midnight ritual draws near
The rambling crowd
Blocks our short-cut home.

"Go get it. Money, money, money.
You greedy fools!"
A loud drunken remark
From a stingy soul.

Do you hear what I hear?

"Get a life. Stop being a pest,
You lazy so and so!"
A soft stern reply
From an up-tight cop.

Do you see what I see?

"Why so nasty?
Why unload one's frustration
On the meekest?"
You say—

I say—
"So it has been,
So it will
Always be."

The church bell rings in the snow.
Here it is! In thunderous roars,
Following the crystal globe's descent,
A new year arrives.

Do you think what I think?

"Time marches on, people too.
Here to stay,
Gone tomorrow!"
You say—

I say—
"What else is new?
Everything changes,
Nothing changes!"

Quiet snow piles up below store signs
And reflects in multi-colors.
Ceaseless energy quickens once again
From the city's four corners.

Our old shoes step
Into a new day.
Our old dialogue raises
Us to face a new plane.

Do you feel what I feel?

Reaction

Besides entertaining us with
Endless moments of pleasure,
A work of great truth and value

Be it a song, a book, a poem,
A painting or a building—
Often, it carries away our beguiled mind

With emotional immunity and
Reduce us to ruminate, laugh or cry,
Perhaps learn and

Be humbled by it.

(Reaction to a friend's bad architecture design)

In Protest

Ostensibly intrusive.
All afternoon, the new scraggly clouds
In freezing air, aim to cajole the sanctimonious
Sun to a juvenile fun of "hide and seek."

Arguably improvised.
The irascible northern wind joins 'n speeds up the
Game's action. Chaos, riot, ensued. The sun hurls
Hail, sleet, snow, in all directions, as it retreats.

Perplexedly neglected.
The hills; grey 'n songless. Tree trunk; nude 'n scaly.
Skinny branches, shaking like a preacher's finger that
Points to those who rule the sky in perfidy 'n howl:

"It's mid April. No more betrayal.
Give us warmth 'n nourishment.
Some need urgent care.
We all need love, or we'll perish."

In secret soil, the signs of Spring stir. Yet,
Timid green sprouts, pink flower buds refuse
To exhibit their opulent designs,
Just to face the murderous atmosphere.

Words Without a Melody
(Unreasonableness)

I heard that song before,
With that familiar word 'n similar tune,
Lamenting love's betrayal 'n revenge.
Puccini immortalized it, Callas lived by it.
Happy in love bears ephemerality.
Sorrow for love stays.

The sun's charm guarantees but uncertainty.
Volcano has its schedule to be coy.
Truth alters from tongue to tongue.
"Matters of heart" links fantasy to abstraction—
Forever means yesterday, one counts as
One of many. Love's sad song lingers.

I saw that tender image before,
With that shadow of lovers strolling
Behind the scented moonlight patch.
As embraces yet to disturb the ground
His fingers strive to gain time's slower beat.
His disparaging eyes break into unreasonableness:

"Open your door, dear lady,
Open your door 'n let me in.
I want to tell you that—
Your love heals
My wounds of desire.
Your smiles tantalize
Me with new value,
Your dream bewitches
But my single dream.

Open your arms, dear lady,
Open your arms 'n let me in your embrace.
I want to tell you that—
Health 'n wealth can wait.
I've nothing
But my heart to serve.
I've everything
To dispel the accusatory feat

Open your heart, dear lady,
Open your heart 'n let me in your warmth.
I want to tell you that—
Oh, let your need be my focus.
Let your touch touch me
With privilege.
OR! Or ——

I sensed that flash of lightning before,
With that cruel break in mind's game.
The masquerade falls away.
As the leaves quiver in red, their
Evening prayer alters to moans. High up
The moon turns without exhortation.

(After Mendelssohn—Song Without Words)

Words from My Reflection

All hatreds spiral up just to be crashed down,
Some tears run aside at a loss,
A jealousy crawls first, then attacks like
All gossips which harbor the predator's brain.
Some go-getters ignore poor men's hands, with
A pernicious tongue to sweep rich men's tedium.

Mocking power, things unfold to rich men's grasp—
Comfort, beauty, fame 'n a doctor's degree......
Bearing power, entitlement denies rich men's claim—
Sensitivity, respect, bravery 'n sacrifice......
The law imposes not to balance each merit,
A thing earned through personal pain seems sweeter.

Love carries the strife of sweet pain,
It propels all the reasons to live.
A wish weaves dreams that
Prefer to look radiant in the air.
Luck rejoices in wish,
Love rejoices in dreams.

To seek clarifies the log.
"Seek and you'll find." So they say.
"Finding the key to equilibrium dulls
All the other acquisitions." So you say.
And, what have you done......no,
No, what have I done today?

Citizen's Rights

We demand our city to
Lower its noise decibels.

We charge the teacher's inability
That causes our children to fail.

We condemn police brutality 'n protest against
Racial unbalance incarcerations in our youth.

We fear the city's –
        Polluted water,
        Poisonous air,
        Judiciary corruption,
        Civil servants' ethics,
        Street crime, child molestation,
        Terrorists from the sky 'n underground,
        Dirty bomb, nuclear missile, war,
        WAR!

Have we to clean up our
Portion of the sidewalk?

(To whoever complains about everything)

Good-byes

There are the last days of **spring**,

The sound of evening rain knocks
On my closed window regardlessly—
      Not like the noise of a **summer** storm,
      Nor like **autumn's** weeping complaint,
      Nor a howling **winter** white-out.
It's like the footsteps that circumspectly
Tread on a paved walkway—
Tap, tap......Tap, tap......
Tap, tap......All night long,
Through the forlorn dampness.

By midnight, I reach out to Debussy 'n
Cover my eyes with his moonlight, sea,
Bells, goldfish, garden in the rain......

Words fail me to respond to the sense of loss.
Tapping the dark window pane to coincide
With the sound of rain drops.
Tap, tap......Tap, tap......Thus,
I share the way **spring** says good-byes.

Beginning and End

I. Open

The beginning celebrates the birth of an idea
That flashes with action 'n hope.
Ignited by need,
Driven by invocation,
No time 'n labor spent, considered vulnerable.
The amount of satisfaction at hand,
Depends upon the amount of care
To percolate the collected realization.

Determination takes the first step,
Gallantry chases fear away,
Individuality points toward virtue.
Be learned like a sponge,
Be discretionary like a needle,
The accomplishments compete with heights.
Conviction encourages them.
Presumption forbids 'n fails.

II. Close

The end concludes all the evidences of
A factual or imaginary adventure—
      The last word on the last page.
      The final curtain call.
      Dried tear marks after a decided parting.
      The kiss of love before burial.
Life's summations come in pairs;
Good or bad, happy or sad, success or failure.

The end doesn't end in some people's minds.
The insecure souls trust angels, devils, heaven 'n hell.
Others study nature's big scheme of things—
Everything created ends. Too, our sun. Works by
Bach, Shakespeare, Picasso, Frank L. Wright,
Marilyn Monroe, 'n I.B.M., B.M.W., K.F.C., —
All'll turn to dust. "What a waste!" I say.
"Un-necessarily necessary! It's nature's way!" I think.

A Night at Lincoln Center

The satisfaction derived from
Witnessing others' misfortunes has
The exclusivity to human, who perfects
It as an art form for entertainment.

The doors swung open.
By their noisy whispers 'n tardy exit,
The Met's audience has experienced
The immensity of a tragic opera.
Triggered by morose 'n delectation,
They stepped into the grip of wintry air.

Lincoln Center exhales by midnight.

Earlier tonight, Puccini's music
Traded tears with the cavernous hall.
Madama Butterfly died in magnanimity.
Spotlighted alone on Met's stage,
A dagger fleshed. She eviscerated her
Young soul for the lover's betrayal.
Though, mendacity permeated throughout
Her life, Butterfly's reply to cruelty
Exceeded humility 'n superiority.

The plaza's fountain glows in eeriness.
The water jets dance with intervals.
I sense the bitterness from their insouciance.
Just hours ago, they received admirations
From the same people who now brush by
With a different frame of mind.

Humblest Ingredients

The skilled chefs hurry 'n at ease,
Sumptuousness of varied dishes emerges
From the humblest ingredients.
Arts beg the hand of knowledge.

To be an opera singer or a hockey player,
The great expectation demands focus.
Talent is a gift,
Experiences produce.

Time's cruelty manifests in choice.
Temptations of desire with
Stains of envy, avarice, regret...
Which sabotage us to abandonment.

We are made of humblest ingredients—
Physiologically speaking.
Whoever, the vision installed,
Differentiates the have 'n have not.

Pen

When a pen opens its eyes,
The dots 'n lines run from
Chaos to chronology, seeking the
Event's metamorphosis 'n logic,
Perhaps the truth.

When a pen opens its heart,
The passion floods with imaginations,
The narration's fractured syntax aims to
Emphasize the ingenuity 'n predilection,
Perhaps a multi-dimensional truth.

Words 'n lines bear the
Pedagogic mystery, for which
The pen tools 'n refines—
To connect 'n to disclose.
To harmonize with contradictions.

Holding a civilization's passage,
Absent of pen's enablers,
Love, hate, war 'n peace, stay silent.
Quantum theory, super-nova, inscrutable,
Arts can't reflect the ugly 'n the beautiful.

Approaching octogenarian,
My pen surrenders to nostalgia.
It seeks topics of guiltlessness
With Peanuts' friends 'n the dog,
Hemingway's Cuba 'n the big fish...

Time guards my memory.
Sing, silver moon of Chungking,
Repeat "twinkle, twinkle, little stars"
Tenderly, as when I was little,
As now, when I put my pen to rest.

There You Are
(For Michael Opest)

There you are
in the middle of N.Y.C's
epidemic of vanity and disregard.

Your homogenized drive to find answers
can hardly match the big city's
hard drive in warped exhibition.

The rain of deception, down from the
fashionable skyscrapers, spreads a seductive
wetness onto those who are bewildered and altruistic.

A spotlight searches for opportunity.
Your eyes shine like a garden, when
the light chases away the darkness
that has shrouded your spring.

"Good-bye," when you utter this time,
it has a touch of day-break energy.

In seclusion, be right, to constitute
new air for the unending brain storm.
To proclaim a planned map, be wise, by
going away and then return empowered.

Details in the original words make a scholar.
We dream for the love of dream,
The goal aims at the foundation of dream.
The action is to locate the parts missing.

Next,
when cheers of the goal reach beyond Mars,
the dream is to have sushi on Jupiter.

A Suicide

He loved the concept of love.
His wife was the love's focus.
A sense of satisfaction
permeated their home with
the love's sweetness.

Less than three years,
like the hot air balloons
busted in cold air, his
wife reneged on her
sacred marriage vow.

The divorce, an opportunistic thief,
robbed him emotionally naked and
exposed his guilt, regret 'n desperation...

"He took it like a man."
His folks boasted, "He's but 35."
But, the pain became thousands of
maggots feeding on his eroded head.

The choices to resolve on the
"matters of hearts" were few to him...
indifference, revenge, alleviation...
They all meant death and
that's exactly what he chose.

A raging pistol in
an inexplicable mouth.

Row and Roll

I row on the water of my belief.
I roll in the letters from library shelf.
A door stands to defend boundaries and
Refine the term private from public.

I gain to proclaim position in public.
My heart is court room in private,
the plaintiff, defendant 'n judge are one.
The crime is a betrayal of naivety,
the accuser is my conscience,
the judge's wisdom transmutes letters
from the library shelf. A belief.

I vocalize with virtue within my comfort zone.
I intrude the dark without a behavior code.
Time owns the space.
The space is guarded by:
Constant
Command
Competence
Congeniality
Code and
Comfort.

I sing to Walt Whitman's patriotic whim.
I fear Tennessee Williams' mendacious ghost.
Civic disorder wears an interchangeable smile.
The candle of faith poisons us before it dies.

So—
We memorialize yesterday.
We demand a faster tomorrow.
Today, we bury our secrets and
gossip about others' shame.

Gossip has no horizon,
like an ant's view to a
tray of stale cakes.

Rapturous Spring

By the promenade's gentle bend
Sandwiched between rose bushes
Two ardent people-watchers
Sit on a park bench
Flutter as they converse

The left one, with a new bouffant hairdo
Waves her arm of jingly bracelets
Avoiding a pestering fly who persists
Finding her perfumed ensemble of
Red dress, purse and shoes as food

The other, with similar silvery coiffure
Tilts toward the sun, looking into
Her jeweled compact mirror
To apply additional rouge
Intently on her lined face

Last night's storm departs in triumph
The ponderous wind, now, meek by morning air
Dotted on the pavement
Fragments of landscape shine
In the reflection of rain puddles

Champagne pink sod
Pinkish purple bough
Purplish yellow leaves
Yellowish pink blossoms, all
Announce the grand entrance

Of an impetuous but rapturous spring.

La Rondine

Reading his travels as a logger,
Gary Snyder's poems, in precise details,
have inspired me by his passion towards the
unspoiled land and a romantic way of life.

In the library on 42nd Street,
The grandiose reading room projects a
mysterious air. It seems that angels ring in
silence to guide the sparks of new connections.

Her blue eyes turn bluer as I steal glances.
She sits diagonally from me across the long
oak table. Laughing in a whispering tone,
"You look tormented, like a real victim,
sitting there scratching your forehead."

"No, I'm just carried away by the hypnotic
subject in the poems." I close the book.

"Do you read Hart Crane, Ashbery or
Garcia Lorca?" Her openness startles me.
"I find them abstruse and puzzling, don't you?"
Is she trying to test me?

"We all enjoy the perplexed phrasing in poetry.
If every stanza becomes a riddle, it kills my
enthusiasm. The content and skill to manipulate the
structure in writing are both significant. I tend to
seek what a poem contains or suggests." With all
the sincerity, but my eyes twitch untimely.

"I love Emily Dickinson 'n W. Carlos Williams.
(Then, they are everybody's favorites.) When I'm
blue, their words are my aspirin." She pays no
attention to what I've said, just rambling on…yet
her feminine charm insists to lure me and captivate my
fantasy.

"I think Robert Creeley was another fine poet. He
disliked opulence or any adornments……" She starts
again.

"Yes, indeed." I interrupt her, trying to stir the
conversation to my advantage. "I like many of
his love poems, so deeply touching in so many
ways, clever and funny too."

She raises her left fingers to comb her light brown
hair. There shines the wedding ring. "Oh, you
are married." I apologize with disappointment.

"Nah, it's just a decoy to fend off the pests."

"You sure are heartless." I try to tease.

"I know what I am." Her mood is now reflective.
"I study. I know what I like. If I discuss literature
or music, those one-track-minded fools never listen to me."

"Listen! I'm listening." I feel embarrassed.

The winter sun casts an artful glow on her.
The vast room recedes behind the long shadows.
A sudden bravery takes over my hesitation.
"Well, it's almost 4:30. Would you like
to join me for a cup of coffee?"

"......" She looks at me then at her watch.

The seconds stretch on like a life-long rehearsal
And my whole life reduces to these few seconds.

"Gee......Great!" She pouts her lips: "But, it'll
have to be a short one. I've promised an early
dinner with Tom and Dick. Then, by 7:30,
Harry'll take me to Met's new production of
Puccini's *La Rondine*.

A Trying Time

She peels off a banana halfway,
as a burlesque queen undresses.
Quickly she takes a bite of its tip.
Her tongue wiggles impetuously to catch
the pulsating sweetness, with her face
unfolding a sensuous pain. Then, examining
the surroundings and her fruit playfully,
she is ready for the next coquettish bite...

"Stop it! Just stop it! You act like a tramp."
Her husband yells.

"Scared? What's wrong? You used to love it,
and begged me for more." Her voice quivers.

"Yea, that was 30 years ago. You didn't wear
dentures 'n your lips didn't wrinkle up like
a bird's nest." He sneers at her.

"Oh, excuses, excuses, you bald-headed, fat pig!
What's the point of trying? I'm just so tired."
She goes upstairs, without cleaning the dining table.

The Wizard of Oz is on TV full blast. He
likes Judy Garland, but after 3 bottles of sweet
wine, he doesn't hear a note of her.

Once More

Love is an enemy to
all that I've owned.
Setting the rules,
selecting methodically,
little by little, love discards
my world and whispers:
"love me, me alone."

For no fault of mine
(or maybe my fault)
little by little, I collect
surreptitiously once more.

I've found my old hobby,
my pride, my foibles, 'n
the feeling of security.

Love loves not
and is gone.
I'm alone once more,
for disobeying the
impossible rules.

Biography of a Stud

At age 12,
a neighborly matron lassoed him
with candies and molded
him into a stirring stud.

At age 22,
he could pick any
young girls as his
reputation 'n scandals grew.

At age 32,
deep in his brain, he begged
only for the thrill that that
first matron could give.

At age 42,
being an international porno star
for 20 years, he took his life.
In heaven and hell, he searched
for that sweet and sour beginning.

This Side of Thirty

She raised her head
In the stillness on the dark mountain
Dried tears marked her face
Her eyes caught at a wrathful judge
A painful sign, a joyless relief
She suffered the ultimate sentence

Stretched out in trembling air
A sudden panic overtook her
She hesitated
She wanted to cry
Then, with a forceful leap
She vanished in a deep ravine

Born in the rain of dust and fire
During Japanese bombing raid in Chungking
She was the youngest child
Of her mother's seven
At fourteen left behind in confusion
While fleeing the surge of Communism
And with no knowledge that
Her family prospered in Taiwan
Classified as an inferior
She grew, survived a loveless marriage
Seeing no possible light
At end of any tunnel
She resolved to end it all

She was just this side of thirty

One Dimensional

Words are one dimensional.
If they're not, by action followed,
their intentions remain intangible.
So,
"I love you"—when whispered, the
next act should produce consequence.

Your finger touches my lips.
My lips search the warm
spots of your anticipation.
Our arms are interlocked,
my longing to belong is
guaranteed by your sweat
and closeness. When the sun begins
to flutter 'n retreats from exhortation,
our hearts find the rhythm
to heavenly harmony.

"Oh, I love you, I love you."
You yell without restriction.
Then, you talk about the moon,
your garden, your plan for a
future breast augmentation.

I close my eyes in fatigue and
drift into the images of food—
beer with a big pizza, buttery
French toast, two fried eggs 'n
home fries with lots of ketchup.

The Good Guy

Night and Day.
Rain or Shine.
The street corner's traffic signal
flashes between—Walk and Don't walk.
                    Don't walk and Walk.
His guilt is in the way
of confessing, towards her,
his true feeling, which oscillates
between—Bitter and Sweet.
                    Sweet and Bitter.

Time has ignored them.
Days march on without their footsteps.
By June this year, their fourth
child will be on its way.
Next, maybe they'll get married.

"Had I not hooked up with
her in college, I could have
been an architect, a painter or
even a race-car driver. All I needed
was a little practice——Right?
                    Right?
Driving a city bus for 8 years now.
Hell, I don't know what's becoming of
me or whom to blame—Oh! Look!
                    Look! Oh!
Ohhh! Such beautiful babies I have here.
Listen, talk is cheap. I just survive by
—Work and Sleep.
    Sleep and Work.
    Work and Sleep."

Epigram in Five Parts

I. The Commuters

In the morning
the commuters in traffic jam
converge to N.Y.C. from all directions
with indoctrinated ambitions
and simmering rage.

By the roadside
the single-filed soldier ants
who overcome hardships and self-pride
follow their scout's
one spotted kill.

II. Cherry Blossoms

The predicted storm
arrived at 3 am. With
thunder and lightning like the
night scenes of a war movie. Worst,
the strategic wind gnashed 'n shook
my house as it quivered to surrender.

When morning sun came up,
everything looked fresh and polished
save the two Japanese cherry trees.
Greenish bald now, with all the
blossoms spread on the front lawn,
made it pinkish red and surreal.

"I've enjoyed these flowers every year.
Oh, how I'll miss them." Complaining to
my neighbor, I hoped for her commiseration.

"Let's put it this way; after few days they'll be
the organic fertilizer for your starving grass."

I nodded,
not sure if that's not neighborly.

III. Long Fur Coat

"I must have this fur coat for my birthday,"
She says to her husband at Bergdorf.

"Dear, it's immoral to kill animals just to
wear their pretty skins." He repeats what he
sees on TV, smilingly. "By the way, last year,
I bought you a long mink one."

"Oh, this is a short one. A fashionable red fox.
Look, it needs much less skins."

"Cruelty! Cruelty! Well, have this one and
trade in the long one." Again, smilingly.

"No, N.Y. gets freezing cold in the winter.
Besides, everyone in our charity group
has a long fur…Without one?
I can't embarrass you like that.
For God's sake!"

IV. Many Colors
(for Martha and Gamal El Zoghby)

Should I spend another dreary day
alone with my tattered thoughts?
The black clouds hanging low to spy
on my every move, while I look for
my mother's eyes to warm my eyes.

I've learnt that silence has many colors.

Oh! In Mozart's merriment, I taste bitterness.
He danced his discontent, sang our agony.
Oh! Should I not love Pollock's frustration
and vulnerability, even if his ego forbids?
Oh! Robert Lowell, how your words encroach
on me. May I not follow your path to doom?

Why did "look" lead me high and gloomy?
What did anger teach me in my father's eyes?
Oh! Why do words appear illegible when
I struggle to be candid?

V. The Game
(for Haner Yang)

The game, no more.
I've been searching for my parents
in the sky, behind the doors,
back to times behind my eyes,
at the life before my reach.

I know they were dead, sir.
I'm not out of my mind.

You see; it's just that I left home
too young 'n too soon.

They loved to play "hide and seek"
with me, while I learnt to walk.
The wars have scattered their scents,
my heart beats keep the secret place.

I'll find them,
I'll find me.

Printed in the United States
136242LV00001B/1/P